tutu

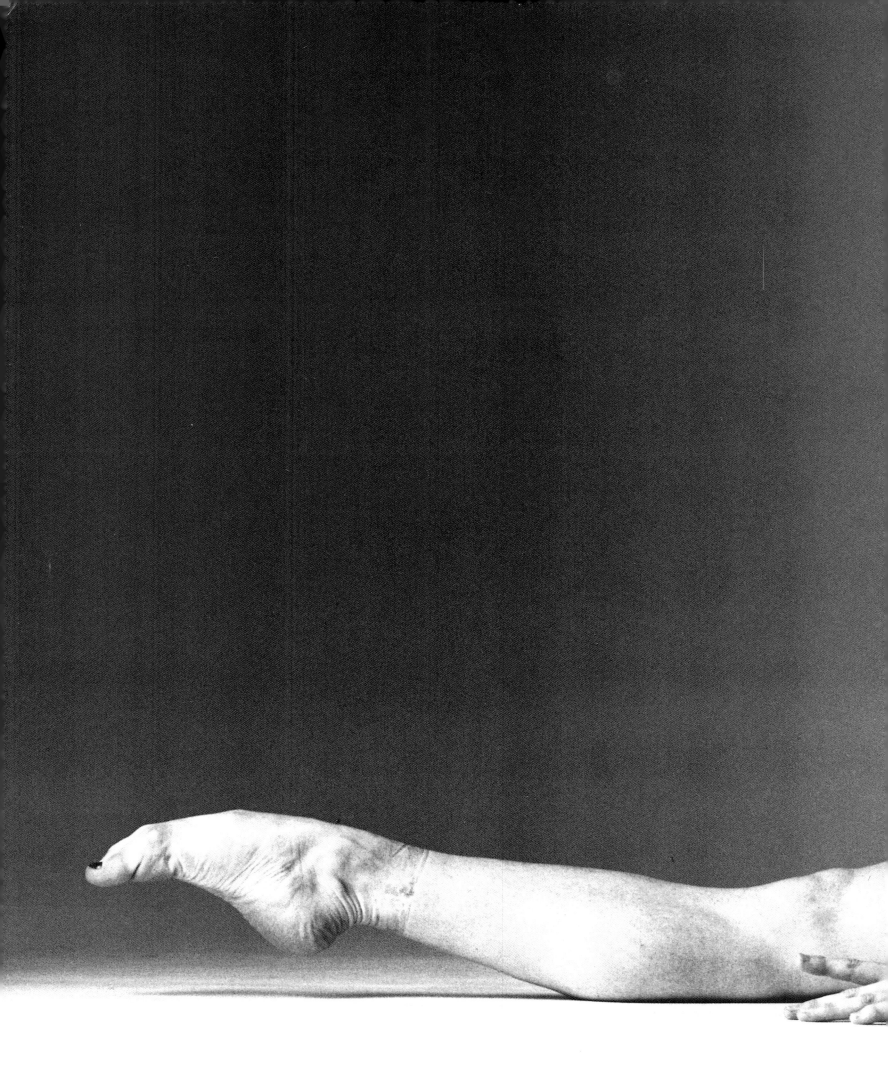

tutu

Greg Barrett

A Sue Hines Book
ALLEN & UNWIN

I dedicate this book to my mum,
Dulcie May Barrett.
(And to my dancing teacher,
wherever he is, whoever he was)

Copyright text and photography
© Greg Barrett 1999

First published in 1999
A Sue Hines Book
Allen & Unwin Pty Ltd
9 Atchison Street
St Leonards, NSW 1590, Australia
Phone: (61 2) 8425 0100
Fax: (61 2) 9906 2218
E-mail: frontdesk@allen-unwin.com.au
URL: http://www.allen-unwin.com.au

National Library of Australia
Cataloguing-in-Publication entry:

Barrett, Greg, 1943 –   .
    Tutu.

    ISBN 1 86508 083 7.

    1. Australian Ballet – Pictorial works.
    2. Ballet dancers – Australia – Pictorial works.
    I. Australian Ballet. II. Title.

792.80994

Designed and typeset by
Deborah Brash/Brash Design Pty Ltd
Photography by Greg Barrett
Photographic prints by
Brent Spencer Young/The Sydney Darkroom
Printed by South Wind Production (Singapore)

10 9 8 7 6 5 4 3 2 1

The Australian Ballet

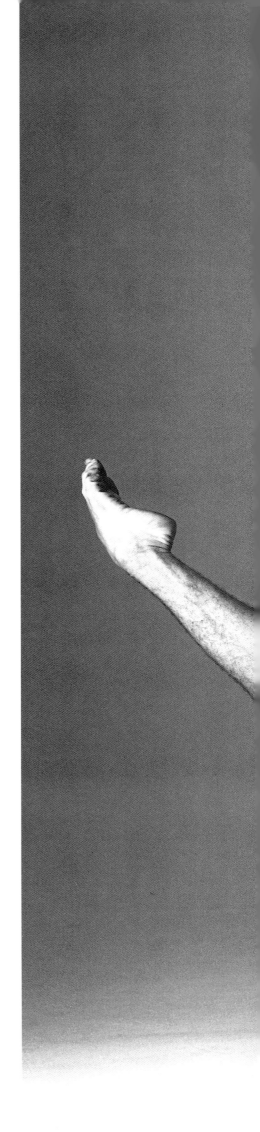

a monologue
with the
photographer

WH Y a book of dancers from The Australian Ballet? Where did it start?

Pierre Bonnard once said that the best thing about museums was the windows. That's so refreshing, isn't it? Well, there seemed to me to be something of the musty smell of the museum about much of the photography I had seen of ballet. I'm tempted to say that often I found it rather reverential. It was my hope that we might open a window and let some air in, stir up the dust a bit.

So the book started with an idea that became an obsession. Martha Graham put it wonderfully when she said that it was as if the concept fastened itself to you like a parasitic growth. Rather than a job, photographing dancers is a compulsive form of behaviour, or so it often feels. So looking at it this way, I haven't had a job for the past 20 years.

Do you work with music in the background when you're making the photographs?

Preferably, no. I usually have the studio as quiet as possible, although it's a collaborative process and sometimes your collaborators may feel more comfortable with music to get them started. During the photographic sessions for this book, after the first five minutes or so no one ever mentioned music again and I usually turned it down or off.

I'd often say to dancers who wanted music that my concern was there would be no music present when people opened the pages of the book. I felt there would be more music in the pictures if there had been none in the studio. And, of course, dance doesn't always have music.

Dance and music can exist quite independently. Sometimes when watching ballet, I wonder how much stronger certain pieces might be without the distraction of music — we look at things differently without music, especially music that is attempting to tell us what to feel. A wonderful quote from John Cage said he wanted to be moved, not pushed!

Does photographing dance take much energy out of you?

A lot! You have to be physically fit to do it properly, to fully engage yourself in the business of it. It's not physically demanding because you're duplicating the moves of the dancers, I couldn't come close to doing that. But to collaborate most fully, to give the dancer(s) the best opportunity you can, you have to invest a considerable amount of physical effort. I'm not sure where that energy is going, but it would seem like cheating the dancers not to give of yourself in that way.

As with anything, you can't half do it. Perhaps I delude myself that my constant activity in some way assists the dancers, but I know that it doesn't work as well if I'm passive, if I'm not working up a sweat too. I couldn't do it sitting and pointing and shouting orders at people. I'm sure the results would be very unsatisfactory.

It's a bit like showjumping: if you're riding properly and the horse baulks at a fence then you continue on over the fence regardless. You have to believe that your horse is going to jump. You can't work defensively with dancers and get the best results. I can't, anyway.

Do you hope people will see you in the work?

I suppose the more you hide yourself, the more you are in it. Similarly, if you try to run away from something in yourself you become more that thing. I don't think you can show yourself in the way a normal self-portrait shows you, which I'm certainly not seeking to do. It's not my intention to have my stamp all over things. It's more like an interpretation on their behalf.

If there's anything that comes close to a representation of self it's in the photograph of David McAllister, where he's jumping with a hand over one eye. For all sorts of reasons that shot is something like a self-portrait because it represents, for me, a goodbye to a certain part of myself. But it's buried so deep that you'd have to know me well to read it as such. Anyway, I'm not sure it would be interesting to anyone else.

When do you know something is 'right'?

(Laughing) You never know! A friend of mine once said that you never finish a poem, you only abandon it. There's a feeling of something being over and done with, but I can't be much more articulate on the subject than that. I'm not looking for a conclusion, a comfortableness; rather, I'm looking for a certain amount of discord and, when the discord is right, and the visual 'balance' of the shot feels right, I suggest we stop, unless the dancers feel we can go further.

The eye will come to accept the discord (as the ear comes to accept discord in music) and eventually, over time, the discord will begin to dissipate and the photograph will develop its own musty smell and someone will have to come in and open a fresh window. As for the visual 'balance', the best photographs should work just as well if one turns the book upside-down or on its side.

9

What attracted you to becoming a photographer?

I've always felt a bit uncomfortable with the title 'photographer'. And in a strange way I still don't feel as though that's what I am. I always felt that photography was so limited in its means, and the result of all one's efforts so flat, so one-dimensional and so silent! And yet these limitations are perhaps photography's strength: that your hands are so tied.

Paul Klee said, 'My freedom thus consists in my moving about within the narrow frame that I have assigned myself for each one of my undertakings. I shall go even further: my freedom will be so much the greater and more meaningful the more narrowly I limit my field of action and the more I surround myself with obstacles. Whatever diminishes constraint, diminishes strength. The more constraints one imposes, the more one frees oneself of the chains that shackle the spirit.'

How much do you plan shots?

I don't plan the images at all. If I plan anything, it's making sure conditions are as good as I can make them for the dancers: I don't ever keep them waiting, I don't muck about with lighting and technical matters after they've arrived, I check the studio is cool enough or warm enough, the mobile phone is turned off and I'm always raring to go when they come in the door . . . full of trepidation, but raring to go.

Sometimes you have a few images in your head left over from dreams or something and they might be a starting point. But I wouldn't bring along a set of drawings of shapes or be thinking of a piece of existing choreography that I'd seen. That would make things too rigid. It's rather that you're finding the shapes in the doing, not in some abstracted situation before the shoot. And the feel of the shoot, the excitement of the discovery and the collaboration is carried into the photographs.

So you don't feel you're compromised by collaboration?

No, not at all. Collaboration is a liberating business. Especially when you have collaborators such as I had in the making of this book, dancers of extraordinary ability and generosity. Linda (Ridgway), who assisted me, worked shoulder to shoulder with me on all that you see here. She's danced with The Australian Ballet, The Royal Ballet and now with the Sydney Dance Company. The collaboration with her was as seamless as it could be without us becoming a part of each other! I am hugely grateful for her contribution. It would not have been the same book without her.

I collaborated with Graeme Murphy many times before on photography shoots and I will always owe him an enormous debt for his generosity. All of it never discussed, not much said at all. And yet I came away from such experiences having learnt so much and feeling so bloody lucky!

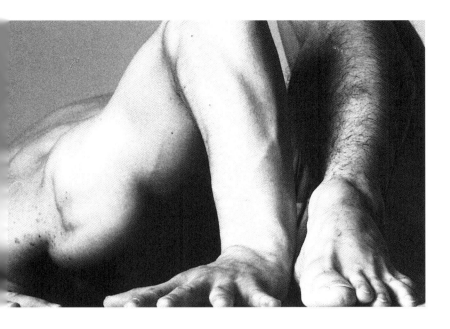

And there are the silent collaborators like Josephine Ridge and Ross Stretton and Sue Hines, who were willing to let us work with absolutely no constraints. They are collaborating by allowing us the space to work within. There was no pressure on us at all in any way. 'It's your book' they said to us over and over again.

Is there someone whom you regard as a mentor?

If the answer has to be in the singular and refer to a photographer, then I'd say Brassai. He had a wonderful and interesting life and he put his energies into so many diverse areas. He wrote fiction and the texts for his own books of photography and drew and was interested in all the arts (and was also uncomfortable, it seems, with the restrictiveness of the label 'photographer'). He was constantly restless and moving on, testing himself in new areas. When once asked late in his life if he was happy, he answered that he couldn't say entirely happy, because he had too many desires.

If there can be more than one mentor I'd include Irving Penn and Harold Cazneaux. Cazneaux was, for me, the greatest Australian photographer. If 'mentor' can include a painter I'd say Bonnard . . . always Bonnard. Not for anything one would see in my photographs, but for his spirit and as an example

of courage in trusting oneself, one's eye, and for his attempt to start afresh each day. I've expressed that clumsily, but it's hard not to feel clumsy around Bonnard. Just as it's hard not to feel clumsy around dancers.

What's the fascination with dancers?

When my work was predominantly in fashion photography the models seemed to become more and more airborne in my photographs. I can remember a Vogue shoot in which I suddenly asked 14 models to jump in the air on a concrete pier out over the Sydney Harbour. Doing this wrote off 14 pairs of Italian shoes . . . I don't think the magazine ever forgave me. Making clothes look good in the air was a great discipline and that helps me now. It's something you can do very badly if you don't apply that discipline, if you get too carried away with the excitement of the moment. It can be intoxicating.

Perhaps you can imagine the excitement I felt working with my first real dancer, who could remember what she had done three moves back and run back through her moves for me again. That was a revelation. Dancers are used to pain

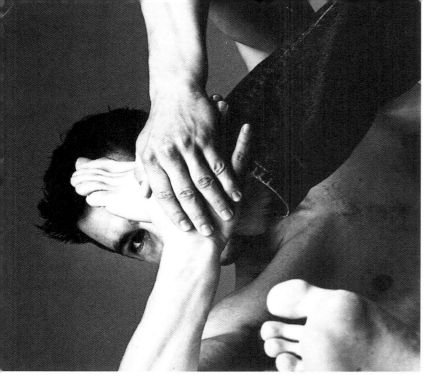

and so they'll not give in until they're happy. In return for this generosity and in respect for them, I try to be as gentle with them as possible, never to waste a single leap or lunge.

During sessions for this book, some of the dancers were heading off to the Sydney Opera House for a performance that same night, so it was more important than ever to be as easy on them as we could be.

I don't think you've adequately answered the question 'why dancers?'.

I don't just photograph dancers. A client whom I think I'm extremely fortunate to have the trust of is the Australian Chamber Orchestra. I've been allowed free reign on their campaigns for the past five years or so and I think I've done some of my best work for them. I photograph opera singers too. And the wonderful Bangarra, the Aboriginal and Torres Strait Islander Dance Company. I still do a lot of portraits and fashion photography. And I direct film. And write.

The pleasure I get from working with performers may be something to do with a traumatic experience in my childhood. I was to sing in an Eisteddfod, but when I got on stage instead of singing, I broke down and wept and had to be assisted off. Maybe I'm slowly edging back onto that stage, facing my

fears. Maybe there's a performer in here who feels better able to perform several stages removed from the actual stage. Photography allows you to do that.

And I find the single-minded discipline of dancers very attractive. It's so single-minded that you may feel excluded from getting close to them. But hopefully, they empathise with your determination to make that fresh, new image with them.

Do other people see you in your work?

I suppose there's inevitably a style that might be recognisable as one's own. I'm not sure how that works and I try not to think about 'style' too often. Being too conscious of such things is a bit like teaching: the danger is that you come to believe the theories you invent about how you did something or why you did something and really, it doesn't happen there at all, in the logical part of the brain. It happens in the oozy part of . . . well, I don't know where.

What sort of equipment do you use?

My equipment is very basic. Most photography assistants who work with me get a great laugh out of it. I have purposely never got into accumulating huge chunks of lighting gear, so I've not felt obligated to use all that accumulated stuff over and over again, or to use a fixed way of lighting things. I use a lot of gaffer tape to hold my lighting inventions together and from the way they look, it's obvious I would make a terrible builder. For this book, I shot everything on one lens (140 mm) on my battered

old Mamiya 6x7. There couldn't be a much worse camera for shooting dance photography because simultaneous with your pressing the shutter button, the camera's mirror flips up, blocking your view of the subject completely. So, in a way, if you saw it, you missed it!

I suspect it's another case of using the minimum, of introducing constraints, as Klee says. To prove something to myself I even took some of the shots in here without looking at all . . . by counting the dancer in and pressing the shutter at the moment I 'felt' would be right. The flash is firing at about a two-thousandth of a second so your timing has to be spot on to catch things at the optimal moment. I don't know where the ability to get that right comes from, particularly in someone as clumsy as myself, but it seems (touch wood) to be present most of the time. If there's a relatively easy bit in the business of photographing dancers, that's it for me.

What training do you have in dance?

None, other than photographing them and going to performances. I can't dance a step myself, I'm hopeless. When I was a child my mum sent me off to dance classes, perhaps to assist me in overcoming my shyness (another traumatic moment comes back to me 40 years later!). The instructor was a man and he used to grab me around the waist and demonstrate the steps to me, which terrified me. I'd hardly been that physically close to my mother! If anyone sees me dancing they should keep well clear . . . I'm dangerous to be around!

I have three dance terms that I know, one of which I pronounce incorrectly, repeatedly. I go to the ballet often, but find the dancing more interesting if I disregard the 'story'. I suspect I am better able to photograph dance if I don't know too much about it.

Ingres said that the most important quality for an artist was naïveté. Well I hope I can continue to maintain my own naïveté in abundance! One can't

manufacture a false naïveté, but you can avoid falling into the trap of being one of the 'cognoscenti', which I suspect could weaken one's work in terms of communicating with a broad audience. So I stick to my three dance terms. And I will never have dance lessons again.

What initially attracted you to photography?

My interest in the visual began with painters like Bonnard and Klee and Ingres, when I was much younger and more confused about what to do in my life. Theirs were the voices that best spoke for me.

Being clumsy, the camera was a revelation. It wasn't until I was 33 that I developed any real interest in photography and then I picked up a camera and could just do it. I've never read a technical book on it; but really, the technical side of photography is not difficult at all. I could teach you all you need to know technically in about an hour . . . the technical side is far too talked up, has far too much of a 'mystique'. But I'm not sure that the other part can be taught. That's the mystery.

For these photographs, I pared the means down to the minimum. One lens. The same lighting all the way through. Minimal props. No trampolines. No manipulation of the images. Very few frames shot of each movement, and so on.

Is having the dancers' trust important?

It's vitally important. Linda was wonderful here. She spoke the language. I was afraid that she might speak the language too well and that I might be excluded from the collaboration, but that didn't happen at all. As I said, it was a most wonderful collaboration. Some of the dancers had worked with me before and I had their trust. Or if I didn't, they certainly acted convincingly. Each shot is like a little relationship. Relationships are nothing without trust, and so it is with this process.

Do you feel that you succeeded in what you set out to achieve?

This will probably sound negative, but you always fail. As we must all fail, I suppose. It's how close we come to succeeding that matters. As a clumsy person with no dance technique, I'm trying to photograph

But you must, after two books and years of photographing dancers, have some understanding of photographic technique?

Well, what is hidden, if we have brought the trick off, is the technique. Technique in dancing (I hope I can speak for dancers here), as in photography, is best learned then pushed back from the conscious mind. There is no time for thinking when you are 'on': you'd be on your face in a moment if all that was guiding you was a consciously followed technique. Using technical words brings technique to the surface, so it's an advantage not to have too many of them and not to allow patterns to be established if you can avoid it. I try to come as close as I can to starting over each time, which can be a bit frightening for some clients. I always feel as though I've just started, that the best is ahead. I hope I always have that. And I hope I always have clients who trust that.

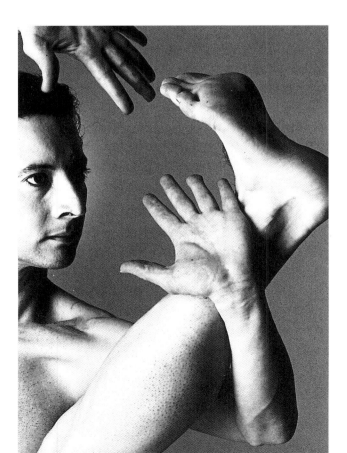

something that I can't do myself. I'm also extremely shy (though I'm told I disguise it well) and yet I love making portraits, although it's an agony. Yeats called it the fascination with what's difficult.

For me, the most challenging dancers were those who were worried about whether they'd succeeded or not, who were still worrying when they went out the door of the studio, who were probably still worrying about it when they went on stage that night. Who are probably still worrying about it now!

I don't think I could judge, with any great objectivity, anyway, whether I've succeeded. But how fortunate am I to have had, in the attempt to succeed, the opportunity to work with people such as the dancers you see here. Perhaps that's success!

Do you ever get stuck for ideas?

Sometimes. And sometimes the way to get things moving again is by changing the form you're using to express yourself.

I was stuck for a form in which to write this foreword. It seemed to be taking almost as long to write as it took to shoot the book! But I felt there were things to be said and things that I needed to try to explain about how the photographs came to be made. But it just didn't want to get itself written, it felt a bit like delivering a sermon. So I thought perhaps I should interview myself. And to make that possible, I made you up. Didn't I.

Yes, you did.

And now we can both step back into the wings and allow the dancers and the photographs to speak for themselves.

Linda Ridgway & Greg Barrett

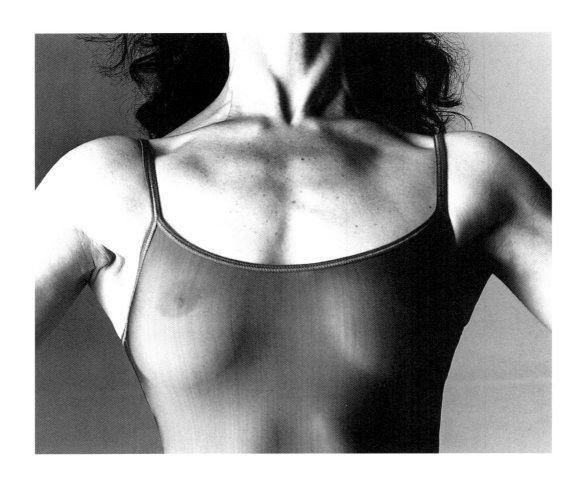

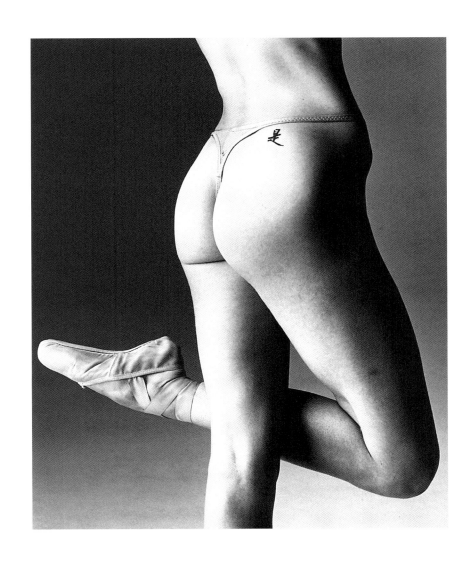

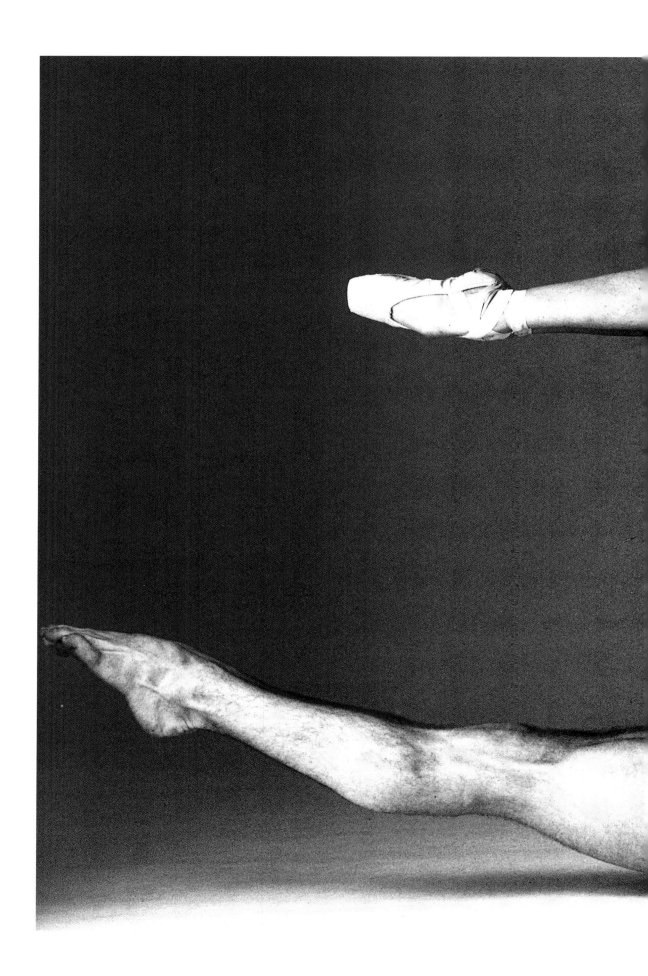

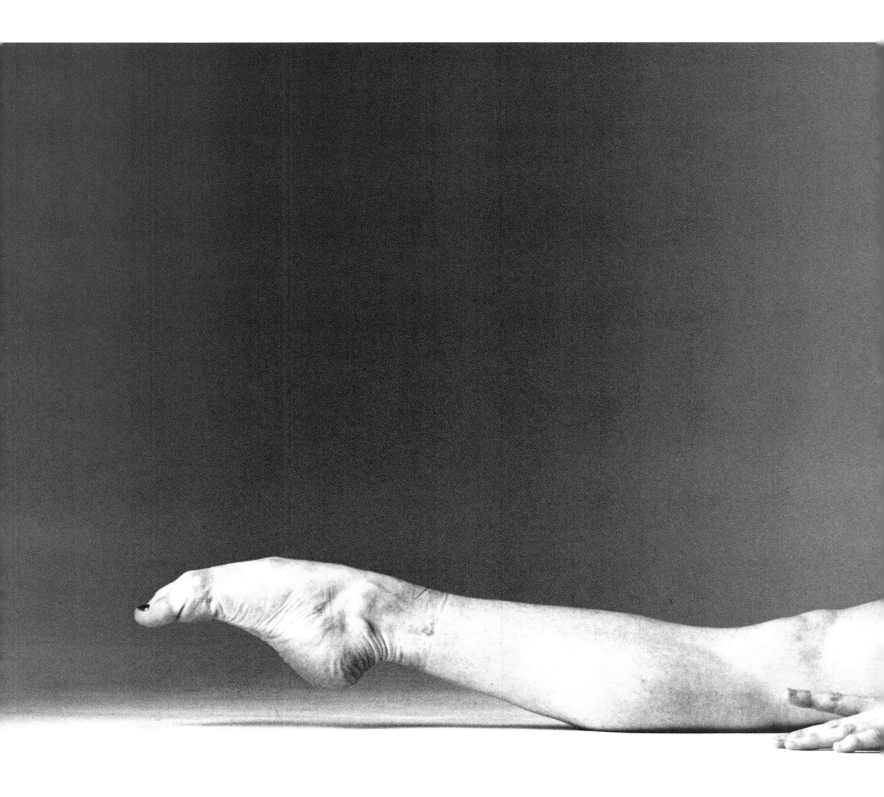

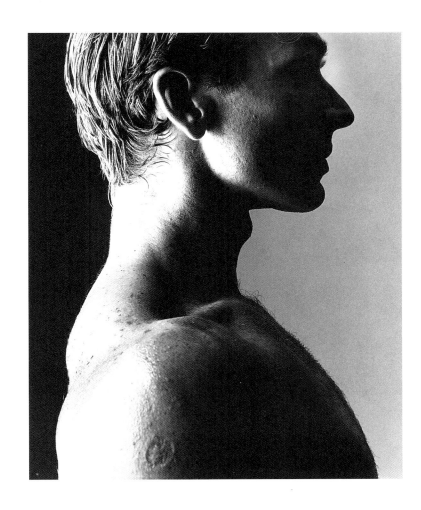

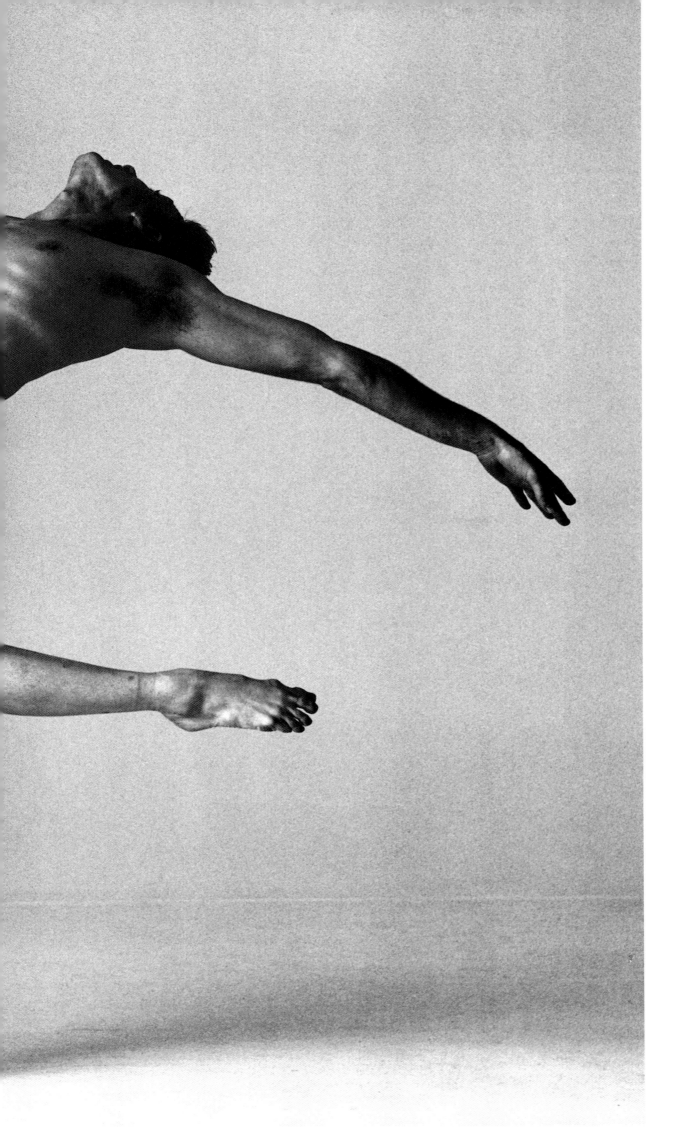

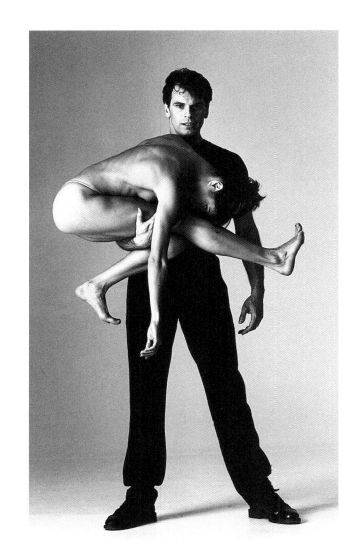

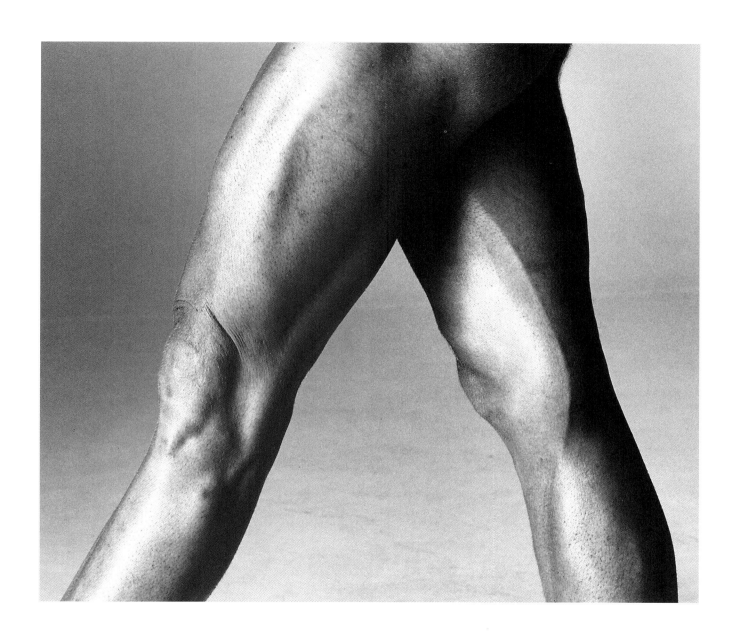

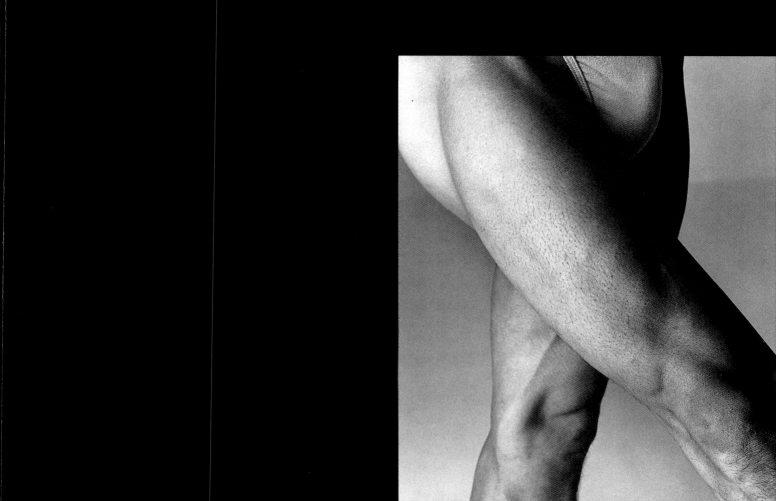

The Dancers

Acknowledgements

Special thanks to:

Deb Brash
Anthony Clarke
Yvonne Gates
Timothy Heathcote
Sue Hines
Debra Howlett
Shirley Kirkwood
Frank Leo
Katie McLeish
Ian McRae
Josephine Ridge
Linda Ridgway
Molly Stacey
George Stroud
Ross Stretton
Maggie Tabberer
Brent Spencer Young

The team at Studio Space
Hair & makeup by Lesley Cameron
Formfit Feelings Body Wear
proudly donated
by Sara Lee Intimates

The Australian Ballet